Unlocking Local Business Success

A Guide To Effective SEO Strategies

BELOMARKETING.COM PRESENTS:

Unlocking Local Business Success
A Guide to Effective SEO Strategies

Introduction

In today's digital age, establishing a strong online presence is crucial for the success of local businesses.

With the right SEO strategies, businesses can enhance their visibility, attract more customers, and ultimately thrive in their communities.

In this guide, we'll explore the key principles of SEO and how they can be applied to boost the success of your local business.

With dedication and a strategic approach to SEO, any local business can thrive in today's competitive digital landscape.

TABLE OF CONTENTS

Section 1: Understanding SEO Basics — Page 7

- Explanation of what SEO is and why it's important for local businesses.

- Overview of key SEO elements such as keywords, meta tags, and backlinks.

- Tips for optimizing website content for local search.

Section 2: Google Business Profile Optimization — Page 19

- Importance of Google Business Profile for local SEO.

- Step-by-step guide to claiming and optimizing a Google Business Profile listing.

- Best practices for optimizing business information, photos, and reviews.

Section 3: Local Keyword Research — Page 33

- Importance of local keyword research for targeting the right audience.

- Tools and techniques for conducting local keyword research.

- Strategies for incorporating local keywords into website content and meta tags.

Section 4: Content Marketing for Local Businesses   Page 45

- Importance of content marketing in driving organic traffic and engagement.

- Ideas for creating high-quality, informative content tailored to local audiences.

- Tips for promoting content through social media, email marketing, and other channels.

Section 5: Building Local Citations and Backlinks   Page 57

- Explanation of what citations and backlinks are and their importance for local SEO.

- Strategies for building local citations on relevant directories and websites.

- Tips for earning backlinks from reputable local sources.

Section 6: Tracking and Analyzing SEO Performance   Page 71

- Importance of tracking SEO performance metrics to measure success.

- Overview of key performance indicators (KPIs) such as website traffic, rankings, and conversions.

- Tools and techniques for tracking and analyzing SEO performance over time.

Understanding SEO Basics

Search Engine Optimization (SEO) is the practice of optimizing a website to improve its visibility and ranking on search engine results pages (SERPs). In today's digital age, SEO is essential for businesses looking to attract organic traffic, increase brand awareness, and drive conversions.

Here's a breakdown of the key components of SEO:

1. Keywords:

Keywords are the foundation of SEO. These are the phrases and terms that users type into search engines when looking for information, products, or services. Conducting keyword research helps businesses identify the most relevant and high-traffic keywords in their industry. These keywords are then strategically incorporated into website content, meta tags, and other on-page elements to improve visibility for relevant searches.

2. On-Page Optimization:

On-page optimization refers to the process of optimizing individual web pages to improve their search engine ranking and relevance. This includes optimizing meta tags (title tags, meta descriptions, and headings), improving website structure and navigation, optimizing images and multimedia content, and ensuring content is high-quality, informative, and relevant to target keywords.

3. Off-Page Optimization:

Off-page optimization involves activities conducted outside of the website to improve its search engine ranking and authority. This includes building backlinks from reputable websites, engaging in social media marketing, and earning citations and mentions from relevant directories and industry publications. Off-page optimization helps search engines determine the credibility and relevance of a website based on its relationships with other websites and online entities.

4. Technical SEO:

Technical SEO focuses on optimizing the technical aspects of a website to improve its crawlability, indexing, and overall performance in search engine rankings. This includes optimizing website speed and performance, fixing crawl errors, implementing schema markup, and ensuring mobile-friendliness and responsive design. Technical SEO ensures that search engines can easily access, crawl, and index website content, leading to improved visibility and rankings.

5. Local SEO:

Local SEO is a subset of SEO that focuses on optimizing a website to appear in local search results for location-based queries. This includes optimizing Google Business Profile listings, earning local citations and backlinks, and optimizing website content for location-specific keywords. Local SEO is crucial for brick-and-mortar businesses looking to attract customers in their local area and drive foot traffic to physical locations.

Conclusion:

SEO is a multifaceted discipline that requires a strategic approach and ongoing effort to achieve success. By understanding the basics of SEO and implementing best practices, businesses can improve their visibility, attract more organic traffic, and ultimately achieve their online marketing goals.

Explanation of SEO and Its Importance for Local Businesses

Search Engine Optimization (SEO) is the process of optimizing a website to improve its visibility and ranking on search engine results pages (SERPs) for relevant keywords and phrases. In essence, SEO aims to make your website more attractive to search engines like Google, Bing, Yahoo, and many others, so they rank it higher in search results when users search for related topics or queries.

Importance of SEO for Local Businesses:

1. Increased Visibility:

When potential customers search for products or services in their local area, they are likely to start with a search engine. By optimizing your website for local keywords, you increase the chances of appearing at the top of local search results, making it easier for local customers to find and engage with your business.

2. Targeted Traffic:

Local SEO helps businesses attract highly targeted traffic from users who are actively searching for products or services in their vicinity. By targeting location-specific keywords and optimizing your Google Business Profile listing, you can ensure that your website attracts relevant local traffic, resulting in higher conversion rates and a greater return on investment (ROI).

3. Competitive Advantage:

In today's competitive business landscape, having a strong online presence is essential for staying ahead of the competition. Local SEO allows small and medium-sized businesses to compete with larger corporations by leveling the playing field in local search results. By implementing effective SEO strategies, local businesses can increase their visibility, attract more customers, and compete more effectively with larger competitors.

4. Enhanced Credibility and Trust:

Studies show that users tend to trust websites that appear at the top of search results more than those that appear lower down. By optimizing your website for local SEO, you not only increase your visibility but also enhance your credibility and trustworthiness in the eyes of potential customers. This can lead to higher click-through rates, more website traffic, and ultimately more conversions.

5. Cost-Effectiveness:

Compared to traditional forms of advertising such as print ads or direct mail, SEO is a cost-effective way for local businesses to reach their target audience. With SEO, you can attract highly targeted traffic to your website without spending a fortune on advertising. Additionally, the results of SEO are long-lasting, meaning that once you achieve high rankings in search results, you can continue to attract organic traffic without ongoing advertising costs.

In summary, SEO is essential for local businesses looking to increase their visibility, attract targeted traffic, and compete effectively in their local market. By optimizing your website for local search, you can improve your online presence, attract more customers, and ultimately grow your business.

Overview of Key SEO Elements

Search Engine Optimization (SEO) encompasses various elements that work together to improve a website's visibility and ranking on search engine results pages (SERPs). Understanding these key elements is essential for implementing effective SEO strategies. Here's an overview of three fundamental SEO elements: keywords, meta tags, and backlinks.

1. Keywords:

Keywords are the words or phrases that users type into search engines when looking for information, products, or services. Incorporating relevant keywords into your website content helps search engines understand what your website is about and when to display it in search results. Key aspects of keywords in SEO include:

- **Keyword Research:** Conducting keyword research to identify relevant keywords and phrases that users are searching for in your industry.

- **Keyword Optimization:** Strategically placing keywords in key areas of your website, such as page titles, headings, meta descriptions, and body content, to improve relevance and visibility.

- **Long-Tail Keywords:** Targeting longer, more specific keyword phrases that have lower search volume but higher conversion rates, often resulting in more targeted traffic.

2. Meta Tags:

Meta tags are HTML elements that provide information about a web page to search engines and website visitors. While there are various types of meta tags, two of the most important for SEO are meta titles and meta descriptions. Key aspects of meta tags in SEO include:

- Meta Titles: The title tag is an HTML element that specifies the title of a web page. It appears as the clickable headline in search engine results and is crucial for both SEO and user engagement.

- Meta Descriptions: The meta description is a brief summary of the content of a web page. While not a direct ranking factor, a compelling meta description can improve click-through rates from search results, indirectly impacting SEO performance.

3. Backlinks:

Backlinks are links from other websites that point to your website. They are one of the most important factors in determining a website's authority and ranking on search engines. Key aspects of backlinks in SEO include:

- Quality and Quantity: Both the quality and quantity of backlinks are important for SEO. High-quality backlinks from authoritative websites are more valuable than low-quality backlinks from spammy or irrelevant websites.

- Anchor Text: The anchor text of a backlink, or the clickable text that users see, provides context about the linked page's content. Optimizing anchor text with relevant keywords can improve the relevance and authority of the linked page.

- Link Building: Proactively building backlinks through strategies such as guest blogging, outreach to industry influencers, and participation in online communities can help improve a website's authority and ranking on search engines.

In summary, keywords, meta tags, and backlinks are three key elements of SEO that play a crucial role in improving a website's visibility and ranking on search engine results pages. By effectively optimizing these elements, businesses can attract more organic traffic, improve user engagement, and ultimately achieve their SEO goals.

Tips for optimizing website content for local search

Optimizing website content for local search is essential for local businesses aiming to attract nearby customers. Here are some tips to help you effectively optimize your website content for local search:

1. Incorporate Local Keywords:

   - Identify and target relevant local keywords that reflect your business's products, services, and location.

   - Include local keywords naturally in your website content, including headings, titles, meta descriptions, and throughout the body text.

2. Create Location-Specific Pages:

   - Develop individual pages on your website dedicated to specific locations you serve.

   - Include location-specific information such as addresses, phone numbers, business hours, and directions.

   - Craft unique and informative content tailored to each location to provide value to visitors.

3. Optimize Google Business Profile Listing:

   - Claim and verify your Google Business Profile (GBP) listing.

   - Ensure all information in your GBP page is accurate, complete, and up-to-date, including business name, address, phone number, website URL, and categories.

   - Encourage satisfied customers to leave positive reviews on your GBP listing to improve visibility and credibility.

4. Utilize Structured Data Markup:

   - Implement structured data markup, such as Schema.org, to provide search engines with additional context about your business, including location, contact information, business hours, and customer reviews.

   - Structured data markup can enhance your website's appearance in search results and increase the likelihood of being featured in local search snippets.

5. Optimize Website for Mobile:

   - Ensure your website is mobile-friendly and responsive to provide a seamless user experience on all devices, including smartphones and tablets.

   - Mobile optimization is particularly important for local search, as many users conduct searches on their mobile devices while on the go.

6. Create Location-Specific Content:

   - Develop blog posts, articles, or landing pages that focus on topics relevant to your local audience.

   - Highlight local events, news, community involvement, and other topics of interest to engage with your local audience and demonstrate your connection to the community.

7. Include Local Business Directories and Citations:

   - Submit your business information to local business directories, review sites, and citation sources such as Yelp, Yellow Pages, and local chambers of commerce.

   - Ensure consistency across all citations, including business name, address, phone number, and website URL.

8. Monitor and Analyze Performance:

   - Regularly monitor your website's performance in local search results using tools like Google Analytics and Google Search Console.

   - Analyze key metrics such as website traffic, search rankings, click-through rates, and conversions to identify areas for improvement and optimize your local SEO strategy accordingly.

By implementing these tips, you can optimize your website content for local search and improve your visibility, attract more local customers, and ultimately grow your business.

Google Business Profile Optimization

Optimizing your Google Business Profile (formerly known as Google My Business) is crucial for improving your online visibility and attracting more local customers. Here are some key steps to optimize your Google Business Profile effectively:

1. Claim and Verify Your Business Profile:

   - If you haven't already done so, claim and verify your business on Google. This process involves requesting ownership of your business profile and confirming your connection to the business through various verification methods, such as mail, phone, or email.

2. Complete Your Business Information:

   - Ensure that all information in your Google Business Profile is accurate, complete, and up-to-date. This includes your business name, address, phone number (NAP), website URL, business hours, and categories.

   - Provide additional details about your business, such as a brief description, services offered, payment methods accepted, and any special attributes (e.g., wheelchair accessibility, outdoor seating).

3. Add High-Quality Photos and Videos:

 - Upload high-quality photos and videos that showcase your business, products, services, and team members.

 - Include a mix of interior and exterior photos, as well as photos of your products, staff, and happy customers.

 - Use relevant keywords in the file names and descriptions of your photos to improve their visibility in search results.

4. Encourage Customer Reviews:

 - Encourage satisfied customers to leave positive reviews on your Google Business Profile. Reviews play a significant role in local search rankings and can influence potential customers' decisions.

 - Respond promptly and professionally to customer reviews, both positive and negative, to demonstrate your commitment to customer satisfaction and engagement.

5. Utilize Google Posts:

 - Take advantage of Google Posts to share updates, promotions, events, and other relevant information directly on your Google Business Profile.

 - Use eye-catching images, compelling copy, and clear calls-to-action (CTAs) to encourage engagement and drive traffic to your website or physical location.

6. Enable Messaging and Booking Features:

- Enable messaging to allow customers to communicate with your business directly through your Google Business Profile.

- If applicable, enable booking features to allow customers to schedule appointments or reservations directly from your profile.

7. Monitor Insights and Performance:

- Regularly monitor insights and performance data provided by Google Business Profile, such as views, clicks, calls, and direction requests.

- Use this data to understand how customers are finding and interacting with your business online and to identify opportunities for improvement.

8. Keep Your Profile Updated:

- Keep your Google Business Profile updated with any changes to your business information, such as new locations, hours of operation, or contact details.

- Regularly review and respond to customer inquiries, messages, and reviews to maintain engagement and ensure a positive customer experience.

By following these optimization tips, you can maximize the effectiveness of your Google Business Profile and improve your online visibility, reputation, and customer engagement.

Importance of Google Business Profile for local SEO

The Google Business Profile (formerly known as Google My Business) plays a critical role in local search engine optimization (SEO) for several reasons:

1. Enhanced Local Visibility:

 - Having a verified and optimized Google Business Profile increases your chances of appearing in local search results, including the coveted "local pack" and Google Maps listings.

 - When users search for businesses or services in their area, Google often displays local results prominently, making it easier for potential customers to discover and engage with local businesses.

2. Information Accessibility:

 - Your Google Business Profile serves as a centralized hub where customers can find essential information about your business, such as your address, phone number, website, business hours, and services offered.

 - Providing accurate and up-to-date information helps users make informed decisions and improves their overall experience, which can positively impact your search rankings and visibility.

3. Trust and Credibility:

  - A well-maintained Google Business Profile enhances your credibility and trustworthiness in the eyes of potential customers.

  - Positive reviews, high-quality photos, and detailed business information signal to users that your business is reputable and reliable, increasing the likelihood of them choosing your business over competitors.

4. Increased Engagement:

  - Google Business Profile features such as posts, messaging, and booking options enable direct interaction between businesses and customers.

  - Engaging with customers through these features not only improves user experience but also signals to search engines that your business is active and responsive, which can positively impact your local SEO performance.

5. Local Pack Rankings:

  - Google's local pack, which typically appears at the top of search results for local queries, showcases a select few businesses relevant to the user's search.

  - Optimizing your Google Business Profile increases your chances of being featured in the local pack, providing prime visibility to potential customers and driving more traffic to your website or physical location.

6. Insights and Analytics:

- Google Business Profile provides valuable insights and analytics about how users find and interact with your business online.

- Monitoring these insights allows you to track your performance, identify trends, and make informed decisions to optimize your local SEO strategy and improve your business's visibility and reach.

In summary, the Google Business Profile is a powerful tool for local SEO that can significantly impact your business's visibility, credibility, and engagement within your local community. By optimizing and actively managing your profile, you can enhance your online presence, attract more customers, and ultimately grow your business.

Step-by-step guide to claiming and optimizing a GBP listing

1. Visit Google Business:

- Go to the Google Business website (https://www.google.com/business/) and sign in to your Google account. If you don't have one, you'll need to create one.

2. Search for Your Business:

- Use the search bar to find your business. If your business appears in the search results, it means that a listing already exists. Click on it to claim it. If not, click on "Add your business to Google" and follow the prompts to create a new listing.

3. Claim Your Business:

- If your business is already listed, click on the "Own this business?" link or "Claim this business" button to begin the verification process. If your business isn't listed, follow the prompts to provide your business information and create a new listing.

4. Verify Your Ownership:

- Google will ask you to verify that you are the owner or authorized representative of the business. Depending on your preferences and eligibility, you can choose from various verification methods, such as receiving a postcard by mail, receiving a phone call, or verifying instantly if eligible.

5. Provide Basic Information:

   - Once verified, you'll be able to access and edit your business information. Ensure that all basic information, such as your business name, address, phone number, website URL, and business category, is accurate and up-to-date.

6. Add Detailed Information:

   - Provide additional details about your business, such as business hours, attributes (e.g., Wi-Fi availability, outdoor seating), and a brief description of your products or services. The more information you provide, the better.

7. Upload Photos and Videos:

   - Upload high-quality photos and videos that showcase your business, products, services, and team members. Include photos of your storefront, interior, products, staff, and any other relevant aspects of your business.

8. Encourage Reviews:

   - Encourage satisfied customers to leave positive reviews on your Google Business Profile. Reviews play a significant role in local search rankings and can influence potential customers' decisions. Respond promptly and professionally to customer reviews to demonstrate your commitment to customer satisfaction.

9. Use Google Posts:

 - Take advantage of Google Posts to share updates, promotions, events, and other relevant information directly on your Google Business Profile.

10. Monitor and Update Regularly:

 - Regularly monitor your Google Business Profile for updates, messages, reviews, and insights. Keep your information accurate and up-to-date, and respond promptly to customer inquiries and feedback to maintain engagement and ensure a positive customer experience.

By following these steps, you can claim and optimize your Google Business Profile listing to improve your online visibility, attract more local customers, and grow your business.

Best practices for optimizing business information, photos, and reviews

Optimizing business information, photos, and reviews on your Google Business Profile is crucial for attracting potential customers and improving your local SEO.

Here are some best practices to help you optimize these elements effectively:

1. Business Information

   - Accuracy and Consistency:
Ensure that all business information, including your business name, address, phone number (NAP), website URL, and business category, is accurate, consistent, and up-to-date across all online platforms.

   - Complete Your Profile:
Provide as much detailed information about your business as possible, including business hours, attributes (e.g., Wi-Fi availability, outdoor seating), and a brief description of your products or services.

   - Use Keywords:
Incorporate relevant keywords naturally into your business description and other sections of your profile to improve its visibility in local search results.

2. Photos and Videos

- High-Quality Images:
Upload high-quality photos that accurately represent your business, products, services, and team members. Use professional photography whenever possible to showcase your business in the best light.

- Variety:
Include a variety of photos, including interior and exterior shots of your business, photos of your products or services in action, staff members, and happy customers. Aim for diversity to provide a well-rounded view of your business.

- Regular Updates:
Regularly update your photo gallery with new images to keep your profile fresh and engaging. Consider uploading seasonal or themed photos to showcase special events or promotions.

3. Reviews

- Encourage Reviews:

Encourage satisfied customers to leave positive reviews on your Google Business Profile. Promptly respond to all reviews, both positive and negative, to show that you value customer feedback and are committed to providing excellent service.

- Engage with Reviews:

Respond to reviews professionally and promptly, addressing any concerns or questions raised by customers. Thank customers for positive feedback and take the opportunity to showcase your commitment to customer satisfaction.

- Monitor Reviews:

Regularly monitor your reviews and address any negative feedback or issues raised by customers. Use feedback to identify areas for improvement and make necessary adjustments to enhance the customer experience.

4. Additional Tips

- Utilize Google Q&A:

Monitor and respond to questions posted by users in the Google Q&A section of your profile. Provide accurate and helpful answers to address common inquiries and improve user experience.

- Utilize Google Posts:

Take advantage of Google Posts to share updates, promotions, events, and other relevant information directly on your Google Business Profile. Use engaging content and clear calls-to-action (CTAs) to encourage user engagement and drive traffic to your website or physical location.

By implementing these best practices for optimizing business information, photos, and reviews on your Google Business Profile, you can improve your online visibility, attract more local customers, and build trust and credibility with your target audience.

Local Keyword Research

Local keyword research is essential for local businesses aiming to improve their visibility in local search results. Here's a step-by-step guide to conducting effective local keyword research:

1. Understand Your Target Audience:

   - Identify your target audience and understand their needs, preferences, and search behavior. Consider factors such as location, demographics, interests, and pain points.

2. Brainstorm Seed Keywords:

   - Start by brainstorming a list of seed keywords relevant to your business, products, services, and location. These are broad terms or phrases that describe what your business offers and the areas it serves.

3. Use Keyword Research Tools:

   - Utilize keyword research tools such as Google's Keyword Planner, SEMrush, Ahrefs, or Moz Keyword Explorer to expand your list of seed keywords and discover additional relevant keywords.

   - Enter your seed keywords into the keyword research tool and analyze search volume, competition, and keyword difficulty to identify high-potential keywords for your local SEO strategy.

4. Consider Local Modifiers:

   - Incorporate local modifiers into your keyword research to target users searching for products or services in your specific location. Examples of local modifiers include city names, neighborhood names, zip codes, and phrases like "near me" or "in [city]."

5. Analyze Competitor Keywords:

   - Analyze the keywords used by your competitors in their website content, meta tags, and Google Business Profiles. Identify common keywords and phrases that are driving traffic to their websites and consider incorporating them into your own local SEO strategy.

6. Long-Tail Keyword Research:

   - Explore long-tail keywords, which are longer and more specific keyword phrases that typically have lower search volume but higher conversion rates. Long-tail keywords can help you target users with specific intent and less competition.

7. Review Google Autocomplete and Related Searches:

   - Use Google Autocomplete and Related Searches to discover additional keyword ideas based on user search queries related to your business, products, services, and location. Pay attention to suggested search terms and phrases that appear as you type in the search bar.

8. Organize and Prioritize Keywords:

- Organize your list of keywords into categories or themes based on relevance and search intent. Prioritize keywords with high search volume, low competition, and clear local relevance.

- Consider creating separate keyword lists for different locations or service areas if your business operates in multiple locations.

9. Refine and Iterate:

- Regularly review and refine your list of keywords based on changes in search trends, user behavior, and business priorities. Continuously monitor keyword performance and adjust your local SEO strategy as needed to optimize results.

By following these steps, you can conduct effective local keyword research to identify relevant keywords and phrases that will help improve your business's visibility in local search results and attract more local customers.

Importance of local keyword research for targeting the right audience

Local keyword research is crucial for targeting the right audience and maximizing the effectiveness of your local SEO efforts. Here's why local keyword research is important:

1. Relevance:

   - Local keyword research helps you identify the specific terms and phrases that potential customers in your target area are using when searching for products or services like yours. By incorporating these keywords into your website content, you ensure that your business appears in relevant search results.

2. Local Intent:

   - Local keywords often include geographic modifiers such as city names, neighborhood names, or phrases like "near me" or "in [city]." By targeting these keywords, you can capture users who are specifically looking for businesses in your local area, increasing the likelihood of attracting qualified leads and customers.

3. Competition:

   - Local keyword research allows you to identify niche or localized keywords with lower competition compared to broader, more generic keywords. Targeting these less competitive keywords can help you rank higher in local search results and stand out from competitors.

4. User Intent:

   - Understanding local search intent is essential for providing users with the information they're looking for. Local keyword research helps you identify user intent behind specific search queries, whether it's informational (researching a topic), navigational (finding a specific business), or transactional (making a purchase).

5. Geotargeting:

   - Local keyword research enables you to create geo-targeted content tailored to the needs and preferences of your local audience. By optimizing your website with location-specific keywords, you increase your visibility to users in your target area and drive more relevant traffic to your website or physical location.

6. Improved Conversion Rates:

   - Targeting local keywords increases the likelihood of attracting users who are ready to take action, such as making a purchase or visiting a physical store. These users have a higher intent to convert, resulting in improved conversion rates and ROI for your local SEO efforts.

7. Enhanced User Experience:

   - By optimizing your website with local keywords, you provide users with a better overall experience by delivering relevant, location-specific content that meets their needs. This enhances user satisfaction and increases the likelihood of repeat visits and referrals.

In summary, local keyword research is essential for targeting the right audience, increasing relevance, and maximizing the impact of your local SEO strategy. By understanding the unique needs and search behavior of your local audience and optimizing your website accordingly, you can attract more qualified leads and customers, drive conversions, and grow your business within your local community.

Tools and techniques for conducting local keyword research

Conducting local keyword research requires the use of various tools and techniques to identify relevant terms and phrases that your target audience is using in local searches. Here are some tools and techniques to help you conduct local keyword research effectively:

1. Google Ads Keyword Planner:

- Google Ads Keyword Planner is a tool that allows you to research keywords and estimate their search volumes. You can use it to find local keywords by entering location-specific terms and filtering results by location.

2. Google Autocomplete:

- Google Autocomplete suggests search terms as you type in the search bar. Use this feature to discover local keywords based on popular search queries related to your business, products, or services in your target area.

3. Google Trends:

- Google Trends provides insights into search trends over time, including geographic data. You can use it to identify trending topics and seasonal fluctuations in search volume for local keywords.

4. Google Search Console:

- Google Search Console provides data on the search queries that are driving traffic to your website. Review the queries report to identify local keywords that users are using to find your website.

5. Local SEO Tools:

- Local SEO tools such as BrightLocal, Moz Local, and Whitespark offer keyword research features specifically designed for local search optimization. These tools provide insights into local search volumes, competition, and ranking opportunities.

6. Location-Based Keyword Modifiers:

- Incorporate location-based modifiers such as city names, neighborhood names, zip codes, and phrases like "near me" or "in [city]" into your keyword research. These modifiers help you target users searching for businesses in specific geographic locations.

7. Competitor Analysis:

- Analyze the keywords used by your competitors in their website content, meta tags, and Google Business Profiles. Identify common keywords and phrases that are driving traffic to their websites and consider incorporating them into your own local SEO strategy.

8. Customer Feedback and Surveys:

- Gather insights from your customers through feedback forms, surveys, or social media interactions. Ask them about the terms and phrases they use when searching for businesses like yours in your local area.

9. Online Reviews and Social Media:

- Monitor online reviews, social media comments, and discussions related to your industry or niche. Pay attention to the language and terminology used by your target audience when discussing local businesses or seeking recommendations.

10. Keyword Analysis Tools:

- Use keyword analysis tools such as SEMrush, Ahrefs, and KeywordTool.io to explore keyword variations, search volumes, competition levels, and related terms for local search optimization.

By using a combination of these tools and techniques, you can conduct comprehensive local keyword research to identify relevant terms and phrases that will help improve your business's visibility in local search results and attract more local customers.

Strategies for incorporating local keywords into website content and meta tags

Incorporating local keywords into your website content and meta tags is essential for optimizing your website for local search. Here are some strategies to effectively integrate local keywords into your website:

1. Identify Local Keywords:

   - Conduct thorough keyword research to identify relevant local keywords that your target audience is using in their search queries. Focus on location-based modifiers such as city names, neighborhood names, zip codes, and phrases like "near me" or "in [city]."

2. Optimize Page Titles:

   - Include local keywords in your page titles to improve relevance and visibility in local search results. For example, instead of simply "Best Coffee Shop," use "Best Coffee Shop in [City]" or "Top Coffee Shop Near [Neighborhood]."

3. Write Compelling Meta Descriptions:

   - Craft meta descriptions that incorporate local keywords and accurately describe the content of the page. Use persuasive language to encourage clicks and provide valuable information to users. Highlight your location and unique selling points to attract local visitors.

4. Include Local Keywords in Headings and Subheadings:

   - Use local keywords in headings and subheadings throughout your website content to reinforce relevance and improve readability. Structure your content logically and naturally incorporate location-based terms where appropriate.

5. Create Location-Specific Landing Pages:

   - Develop location-specific landing pages targeting different geographic areas or neighborhoods you serve. Optimize these pages with local keywords, business information, and relevant content tailored to each location.

6. Incorporate Local Keywords in Body Content:

   - Integrate local keywords seamlessly into the body content of your web pages. Use them naturally within sentences and paragraphs while providing valuable information that addresses the needs and interests of your local audience.

7. Optimize Image Alt Text:

   - Use descriptive alt text for images that include local keywords whenever applicable. This helps improve accessibility for users with disabilities and provides additional context to search engines, enhancing your website's relevance for local searches.

8. Leverage Structured Data Markup:

- Implement structured data markup, such as Schema.org, to provide search engines with additional context about your business, including location-specific information. Use schema markup to mark up your business address, contact details, business hours, and other relevant data.

9. Create Local Content:

- Produce blog posts, articles, or other types of content that are specific to your local area or address topics relevant to your local audience. Incorporate local keywords naturally within this content to attract local traffic and demonstrate your expertise in the community.

10. Monitor and Adjust:

- Regularly monitor the performance of your website in local search results using tools like Google Analytics and Google Search Console. Analyze keyword rankings, organic traffic, and user engagement metrics to identify areas for improvement and adjust your local SEO strategy accordingly.

By implementing these strategies, you can effectively incorporate local keywords into your website content and meta tags to improve your visibility in local search results, attract more local customers, and grow your business within your target geographic area.

Content Marketing for Local Businesses

Content marketing is a powerful strategy for local businesses to attract, engage, and retain customers within their target geographic area. Here's a tailored approach to content marketing for local businesses:

1. Identify Your Audience:

   - Understand your local audience, including their demographics, interests, pain points, and preferences. Consider factors such as age, gender, income level, lifestyle, and purchasing behavior.

2. Create Localized Content:

   - Develop content that is specifically tailored to your local audience and addresses their unique needs and interests. Highlight local events, news, landmarks, and community initiatives to resonate with your audience and demonstrate your connection to the community.

3. Optimize for Local SEO:

   - Incorporate local keywords naturally into your content to improve your visibility in local search results. Target location-specific terms, such as city names, neighborhood names, and phrases like "near me" or "in [city]," to attract local traffic to your website.

4. Leverage Google Business Profile:

- Utilize Google Business Profile to publish posts, share updates, and promote events directly to local customers. Optimize your Google Business Profile listing with accurate business information, high-quality photos, and positive reviews to enhance your online presence and attract more local customers.

5. Produce Engaging Blog Posts:

- Create blog posts that address topics relevant to your local audience and showcase your expertise in your industry. Offer valuable insights, tips, and advice that demonstrate your authority and provide solutions to your customers' problems.

6. Showcase Customer Success Stories:

- Share customer success stories and testimonials that highlight the positive experiences of your satisfied customers. Feature local customers and businesses to foster a sense of community and trust among your audience.

7. Engage with Local Events and Causes:

- Participate in local events, sponsorships, and community initiatives to increase your brand visibility and support local causes. Create content around your involvement in these events and share it with your audience to showcase your commitment to the community.

8. Utilize Social Media:

   - Use social media platforms to share your content, engage with your audience, and promote your business locally. Share behind-the-scenes photos, customer testimonials, and updates about your products or services to keep your audience informed and engaged.

9. Encourage User-Generated Content:

   - Encourage your customers to create and share content about their experiences with your business on social media. User-generated content, such as photos, reviews, and testimonials, serves as authentic endorsements and helps build trust with potential customers.

10. Measure and Analyze Results:

   - Track the performance of your content marketing efforts using analytics tools to measure key metrics such as website traffic, engagement, conversions, and ROI. Analyze the data to identify trends, insights, and areas for improvement, and adjust your content strategy accordingly.

By implementing these content marketing strategies for local businesses, you can effectively engage with your local audience, increase brand awareness, drive website traffic, and ultimately, grow your business within your community.

Importance of content marketing in driving organic traffic and engagement

Content marketing plays a significant role in driving organic traffic and engagement for businesses of all sizes and industries. Here are several reasons why content marketing is important for boosting organic traffic and fostering engagement:

1. Provides Value to Users:

   - Content marketing involves creating and sharing valuable, relevant, and informative content that addresses the needs, interests, and pain points of your target audience. By providing valuable content, you attract users who are actively seeking information or solutions related to your industry or niche.

2. Improves Search Engine Visibility:

   - High-quality content that is optimized for relevant keywords helps improve your website's visibility in search engine results pages (SERPs). Search engines prioritize websites that regularly produce fresh, relevant, and authoritative content, making content marketing a crucial component of any SEO strategy.

3. Builds Trust and Credibility:

   - Consistently publishing valuable and informative content helps establish your brand as a trusted authority in your industry. By providing valuable insights, addressing common questions, and offering solutions to your audience's problems, you build trust and credibility with your audience, which can lead to increased engagement and loyalty over time.

4. Drives Organic Traffic:

- Well-executed content marketing strategies attract organic traffic to your website by targeting relevant keywords, answering user queries, and addressing specific pain points. As users discover and engage with your content through organic search, social media, or referrals, they become more familiar with your brand and more likely to explore your products or services.

5. Increases Brand Awareness:

- Content marketing increases your brand's visibility and awareness by showcasing your expertise, values, and unique selling propositions. By consistently publishing valuable content across various channels, you reach a wider audience and create more opportunities for users to discover and engage with your brand.

6. Enhances User Engagement:

- Engaging and relevant content encourages users to interact with your brand, whether through reading blog posts, watching videos, sharing content on social media, or participating in discussions. By fostering meaningful interactions and conversations, you deepen your connection with your audience and increase engagement levels.

7. Generates Leads and Conversions:

- Effective content marketing strategies drive leads and conversions by guiding users through the buyer's journey and nurturing them with relevant and valuable content. By providing informative content at each stage of the customer journey, you build trust, educate prospects, and ultimately, drive them to take action, such as making a purchase or contacting your business.

8. Supports Customer Retention:

- Content marketing is not only about attracting new customers but also about retaining existing ones. By providing ongoing value and support through valuable content, you keep your audience engaged and loyal to your brand, leading to higher customer retention rates and lifetime value.

In summary, content marketing is essential for driving organic traffic and engagement by providing value to users, improving search engine visibility, building trust and credibility, increasing brand awareness, enhancing user engagement, generating leads and conversions, and supporting customer retention efforts. By investing in content marketing strategies, businesses can effectively reach and engage their target audience, ultimately driving growth and success.

Ideas for creating high-quality, informative content tailored to local audiences

Creating high-quality, informative content tailored to local audiences requires understanding their interests, needs, and preferences. Here are some ideas for generating content that resonates with your local audience:

1. Local Events and Activities:

   - Create content highlighting upcoming local events, festivals, concerts, and community gatherings. Provide event details, schedules, and tips for attendees. Consider interviewing event organizers or attendees to provide insider perspectives.

2. Neighborhood Spotlights:

   - Showcase different neighborhoods or districts within your city or town. Create neighborhood guides featuring local attractions, restaurants, parks, and hidden gems. Include photos, descriptions, and recommendations to help residents and visitors explore their surroundings.

3. Business Spotlights:

   - Feature local businesses, entrepreneurs, and artisans in your area. Interview business owners, highlight their stories, and showcase their products or services. Promote collaboration and support within the local business community.

4. Local History and Culture:

   - Explore the history, heritage, and culture of your local area. Write articles, blog posts, or videos about significant landmarks, historical events, or cultural traditions. Share fascinating stories and anecdotes that resonate with residents and celebrate the unique identity of your community.

5. Community Resources and Services:

   - Compile a list of useful resources and services available in your community, such as libraries, parks, community centers, healthcare facilities, and volunteer organizations. Provide descriptions, contact information, and tips for accessing these resources.

6. Seasonal Content:

   - Create seasonal content tailored to local weather, holidays, and activities. Share seasonal recipes, outdoor activities, gardening tips, or winter safety guides. Tailor your content to reflect the changing seasons and the needs of your local audience.

7. Local News and Updates:

   - Stay informed about local news, developments, and issues affecting your community. Provide timely updates, insights, and analysis on relevant topics such as infrastructure projects, local elections, or community initiatives. Keep your audience informed and engaged with the latest happenings in their area.

8. Community Profiles and Interviews:

   - Spotlight local residents, influencers, or community leaders who are making a positive impact in your area. Conduct interviews, share their stories, and showcase their contributions to the community. Highlight their achievements and celebrate their contributions.

9. Local Sports and Recreation:

   - Cover local sports teams, leagues, and recreational activities happening in your area. Provide game schedules, player profiles, and match highlights. Encourage community involvement and support for local athletes and teams.

10. Tips for Living Local:

   - Offer practical tips, advice, and hacks for living and thriving in your local area. Share insights on transportation, dining, housing, education, and other aspects of daily life. Provide insider tips and recommendations to help newcomers and longtime residents alike make the most of their local experience.

By creating content that resonates with your local audience and addresses their specific interests and needs, you can build a loyal following, strengthen your brand's presence in the community, and drive engagement with your target audience.

Tips for promoting content through social media, email marketing, and other channels

Promoting content through social media, email marketing, and other channels is essential for reaching and engaging your target audience. Here are some tips for effectively promoting your content across various channels:

1. Social Media Promotion

  - Identify the Right Platforms:
Determine which social media platforms are most popular among your target audience and focus your efforts on those platforms.

  - Optimize Content for Each Platform:
Tailor your content to fit the format and audience preferences of each social media platform. Use engaging visuals, hashtags, and captions to capture attention and encourage interaction.

  - Schedule Regular Posts:
Maintain a consistent posting schedule to keep your audience engaged and aware of your content. Use social media management tools to schedule posts in advance and track performance metrics.

  - Encourage Sharing and Engagement:
Prompt your followers to share, like, and comment on your posts to increase visibility and reach. Ask questions, run polls, and encourage user-generated content to foster engagement.

- Utilize Paid Advertising:
Consider using paid advertising options, such as promoted posts or targeted ads, to reach a larger audience and drive traffic to your content. Use targeting options to reach users based on demographics, interests, and location.

2. Email Marketing

- Build a Targeted Email List:
Segment your email list based on factors such as demographics, interests, and purchasing behavior to deliver personalized content to your subscribers.

- Craft Compelling Subject Lines:
Write attention-grabbing subject lines that entice recipients to open your emails. Use personalization, urgency, or curiosity to increase open rates.

- Provide Value in Content:
Offer valuable content in your emails, such as informative articles, exclusive offers, or helpful tips. Focus on providing solutions to your subscribers' problems and addressing their needs.

- Include Clear CTAs:
Include clear and compelling calls-to-action (CTAs) in your emails to encourage recipients to take action, such as clicking through to read a blog post, making a purchase, or signing up for an event.

- Track and Analyze Performance:
Monitor key metrics such as open rates, click-through rates, and conversion rates to evaluate the effectiveness of your email campaigns. Use this data to refine your strategies and improve results over time.

3. Other Promotion Channels

- Collaborate with Influencers:

Partner with influencers or local community leaders who have a strong following and influence in your target market. Work with them to create and promote content that resonates with their audience.

- Engage in Online Communities:

Participate in relevant online communities, forums, and discussion groups where your target audience is active. Share valuable insights, answer questions, and promote your content in a non-intrusive manner.

- Guest Blogging and Cross-Promotion:

Write guest blog posts for other websites or blogs in your industry or niche. Include links back to your own content to drive traffic and increase visibility. Similarly, collaborate with other businesses or organizations for cross-promotion opportunities.

- Attend and Sponsor Events:

Participate in local events, conferences, and trade shows where you can promote your content and engage with your target audience in person. Sponsorship opportunities can also provide exposure to a wider audience.

By leveraging these promotion tips across social media, email marketing, and other channels, you can effectively increase the reach, visibility, and engagement of your content, ultimately driving traffic and conversions for your business.

Building Local Citations and Backlinks

Building local citations and backlinks is crucial for improving your local search visibility and authority. Here's how to effectively build local citations and backlinks for your business:

Building Local Citations

1. Create Business Listings:

   - Ensure your business is listed on major online directories and citation sites such as Google Business Profile, Yelp, Bing Places, Yahoo Local, and industry-specific directories. Provide consistent and accurate NAP (Name, Address, Phone Number) information across all listings.

2. Claim Local Directories:

   - Claim and verify your business listings on local directories, review sites, and platforms relevant to your industry. This includes local chamber of commerce websites, tourism boards, and business associations.

3. Optimize Listings:

   - Optimize your business listings with complete and up-to-date information, including business hours, website URL, categories, and descriptions. Use relevant keywords and location-specific terms in your business descriptions.

4. Utilize Structured Citations:

   - Incorporate structured citations in online business directories, local blogs, news sites, and social media profiles. These structured citations provide search engines with valuable information about your business and help improve your local search rankings.

5. Local Citations Audit:

   - Conduct regular audits of your local citations to ensure accuracy and consistency. Use tools like Moz Local, BrightLocal, or Yext to manage and monitor your citations across various platforms.

Building Backlinks

1. Create High-Quality Content:

   - Develop informative, engaging, and shareable content that resonates with your target audience. This could include blog posts, infographics, videos, case studies, or industry reports.

2. Local Partnerships and Collaborations:

   - Build relationships with local businesses, organizations, and influencers in your community. Collaborate on projects, events, or promotions that offer mutual benefits and opportunities for backlinking.

3. Local Sponsorships and Events:

  - Sponsor local events, charities, or community initiatives and request a mention or backlink on their website. Participate in local sponsorship opportunities that align with your brand values and target audience.

4. Guest Blogging and Contributed Content:

  - Write guest blog posts or contribute articles to local publications, industry blogs, or community newsletters. Include a backlink to your website in the author bio or within the content where relevant.

5. Submit Press Releases:

  - Distribute press releases about noteworthy events, milestones, or announcements related to your business. Submit press releases to local media outlets, newspapers, and online news sites, and include links back to your website.

6. Local Reviews and Testimonials:

  - Encourage satisfied customers to leave positive reviews and testimonials on your website, social media profiles, and review sites. Respond to reviews professionally and engage with customers to build trust and credibility.

7. Monitor Competitor Backlinks:

   - Analyze your competitors' backlink profiles to identify potential opportunities for building backlinks. Look for websites, blogs, or directories where your competitors have been mentioned and reach out to request inclusion for your business.

8. Monitor and Analyze Results:

   - Regularly monitor your local citations and backlinks using tools like Google Search Console, Moz, or Ahrefs. Track the quantity, quality, and impact of your citations and backlinks on your local search rankings and organic traffic.

By implementing these strategies for building local citations and backlinks, you can strengthen your online presence, improve your local search visibility, and drive more traffic and leads to your business.

Explanation of what citations and backlinks are and their importance for local SEO

Let's break down what citations and backlinks are, and why they are essential for local SEO:

1. Citations

Definition: Citations refer to online mentions of your business's Name, Address, and Phone Number on external websites, directories, social platforms, or local listings.

Importance for Local SEO

- Local Ranking Signal: Citations are a crucial ranking factor for local search results. Search engines like Google use citations to assess the credibility, relevance, and authority of your business, particularly for local queries.

- Consistency:
Consistent information across various online platforms reinforces the legitimacy of your business in the eyes of search engines and users. Inaccurate or inconsistent citations can lead to confusion and negatively impact your local search rankings.

- Visibility and Trust:
Citations help improve the visibility and trustworthiness of your business within your local area. When users encounter consistent information about your business across multiple sources, they are more likely to trust your brand and choose it over competitors.

2. Backlinks

Definition: Backlinks, also known as inbound links or external links, are hyperlinks from other websites that point back to your website.

Importance for Local SEO

- Authority and Trustworthiness:

Backlinks serve as votes of confidence from other websites, indicating that your content is valuable and authoritative. High-quality backlinks from reputable websites in your industry or local community enhance your website's credibility and trustworthiness.

- Improved Rankings:

Backlinks are a significant ranking factor for search engines. Websites with a greater number of high-quality backlinks tend to rank higher in search engine results pages (SERPs), including local search results.

- Local Relevance:

Backlinks from local websites, directories, or businesses within your geographic area signal to search engines that your business is relevant to local users. Local backlinks help strengthen your website's relevance and authority for local search queries.

- Referral Traffic:

Backlinks not only contribute to your website's SEO performance but also drive referral traffic from other websites. Users who click on backlinks from relevant sources are more likely to be interested in your products or services, leading to potential conversions.

In summary, citations and backlinks are essential components of local SEO strategies. Citations help establish the credibility and legitimacy of your business within your local area, while backlinks enhance your website's authority, relevance, and visibility in local search results. By actively managing and acquiring citations and backlinks, you can improve your local search rankings, attract more local customers, and grow your business online.

Strategies for building local citations on relevant directories and websites

Building local citations on relevant directories and websites is essential for improving your local search visibility and credibility. Here are some strategies to effectively build local citations:

1. Identify High-Quality Directories:

   - Start by identifying reputable directories and websites that are relevant to your industry and location. Focus on directories that are well-established, authoritative, and frequently visited by your target audience.

2. Claim and Verify Listings:

   - Claim and verify your business listings on major online directories such as Google Business, Yelp, Bing Places, Yahoo Local, and industry-specific directories. Ensure that your business information is accurate, consistent, and up-to-date across all listings.

3. Optimize Listings for SEO:

   - Optimize your business listings with relevant keywords, categories, and descriptions that accurately reflect your products, services, and location. Include important information such as business hours, website URL, and contact details to make it easy for customers to find and connect with your business.

4. Explore Niche Directories:

- Look for niche directories and websites that cater specifically to your industry or niche. These directories may have a smaller audience but can provide highly targeted exposure to potential customers who are actively seeking businesses like yours.

5. Leverage Local Chambers of Commerce:

- Join your local chamber of commerce and leverage their online directory to promote your business within the local community. Chamber of commerce websites often have high authority and trustworthiness, making them valuable sources of local citations.

6. Engage with Local Organizations:

- Partner with local organizations, associations, and nonprofits that are relevant to your industry or community. Many of these organizations may have online directories or member listings where you can showcase your business and build local citations.

7. Seek Out Review Sites and Blogs:

- Identify review sites, blogs, and online publications that focus on your industry or local area. Submit your business for inclusion in their directories or reach out to request coverage or reviews that include citations back to your website.

8. Monitor and Update Citations Regularly:

- Regularly monitor your existing citations and ensure that your business information remains accurate and consistent across all directories and websites. Use citation management tools or services to streamline the process and identify any discrepancies or missing listings.

9. Encourage Customer Reviews and Citations:

- Encourage satisfied customers to leave positive reviews and citations for your business on relevant directories and websites. Offer incentives or rewards for customers who take the time to share their experiences and recommend your business to others.

10. Track Performance and Adjust Strategies:

- Track the performance of your local citations using tools like Google Analytics, Google Search Console, or local SEO software. Monitor key metrics such as visibility, traffic, and conversions to evaluate the effectiveness of your citation-building efforts and make adjustments as needed.

By implementing these strategies for building local citations on relevant directories and websites, you can improve your local search rankings, increase your online visibility, and attract more local customers to your business.

Tips for earning backlinks from reputable local sources

Earning backlinks from reputable local sources is a valuable strategy for improving your local search visibility and authority. Here are some tips for earning backlinks from local sources:

1. Create High-Quality, Localized Content:

   - Develop informative, engaging, and localized content that resonates with your local audience. This could include local guides, case studies, community events, or industry insights relevant to your area. Quality content is more likely to attract backlinks from local websites and blogs.

2. Partner with Local Businesses and Organizations:

   - Build relationships with other local businesses, organizations, and nonprofits in your community. Collaborate on joint projects, sponsorships, or events that offer opportunities for mutual promotion and backlinking. Look for partnerships that align with your brand values and target audience.

3. Participate in Local Events and Sponsorships:

   - Get involved in local events, conferences, fundraisers, or charity initiatives as a sponsor, speaker, or exhibitor. Many event organizers provide backlinks to sponsors on their websites or event pages, providing valuable exposure and local backlinks.

4. Leverage Local Media and Publications:

 - Reach out to local newspapers, magazines, blogs, and online publications to pitch story ideas or contribute guest articles. Offer to share your expertise, insights, or success stories related to your industry or local community. In return, you may earn backlinks to your website or content.

5. Utilize Local Directories and Chambers of Commerce:

 - Join local directories, chambers of commerce, business associations, or industry groups in your area. Many of these organizations offer member directories or resource listings where you can showcase your business and earn authoritative backlinks.

6. Offer Discounts or Special Offers for Locals:

 - Create exclusive discounts, promotions, or special offers for local residents or customers. Promote these offers on your website, social media, and local directories to attract attention and encourage backlinks from local bloggers, influencers, or deal websites.

7. Engage with Local Influencers and Bloggers:

 - Identify local influencers, bloggers, or social media personalities who have a strong following in your community. Reach out to them to introduce your business, offer product samples or experiences, and propose collaboration opportunities that may result in backlinks from their websites or social media profiles.

8. Provide Testimonials or Reviews:

  - Offer testimonials or reviews for other local businesses, products, or services that you have positive experiences with. In return, you may receive backlinks from their websites or acknowledgement in their testimonials section.

9. Host Local Events or Workshops:

  - Organize local events, workshops, or seminars related to your industry or area of expertise. Promote these events on your website, social media, and local event listings to attract attendees and earn backlinks from event promotion websites or local media outlets covering the event.

10. Monitor Local Backlink Opportunities:

  - Regularly monitor local websites, blogs, and directories for opportunities to earn backlinks. Set up Google Alerts for mentions of your brand, industry, or local keywords, and reach out to website owners or bloggers who mention your business to request a backlink or collaboration opportunity.

By implementing these tips for earning backlinks from reputable local sources, you can strengthen your local search presence, increase your website's authority, and attract more local customers to your business.

Tracking and Analyzing SEO Performance

Tracking and analyzing SEO performance is essential for understanding the effectiveness of your efforts and identifying areas for improvement. Here's how to effectively track and analyze SEO performance:

1. Define Key Performance Indicators (KPIs):

   - Identify the key metrics that align with your SEO goals and objectives. Common KPIs include organic traffic, keyword rankings, backlink profile, conversion rates, bounce rates, and engagement metrics such as time on page and pages per session.

2. Set Up Google Analytics:

   - Install Google Analytics on your website to track organic traffic, user behavior, and conversion data. Set up custom reports and segments to monitor specific SEO KPIs and gain insights into how organic search traffic is performing over time.

3. Use Google Search Console:

   - Utilize Google Search Console to monitor your website's performance in Google search results. Track impressions, clicks, click-through rates (CTRs), and average positions for your target keywords. Identify opportunities to improve your website's visibility and clickability in search results.

4. Monitor Keyword Rankings:

  - Use SEO tools like SEMrush, Ahrefs, or Moz to track keyword rankings for your target keywords. Monitor changes in rankings over time, identify keywords with high search volume and low competition, and optimize your content and SEO strategies accordingly.

5. Analyze Backlink Profile:

  - Monitor your website's backlink profile using tools like Ahrefs, Majestic, or Moz. Track the quantity, quality, and diversity of backlinks pointing to your website. Identify new backlink opportunities, monitor for toxic or spammy backlinks, and disavow harmful links if necessary.

6. Assess On-Page Optimization:

  - Evaluate the on-page optimization of your website's individual pages. Analyze factors such as meta tags, headings, content quality, internal linking structure, and page load speed. Optimize your pages for relevant keywords and user experience to improve organic search performance.

7. Track Conversion Metrics:

  - Measure the impact of organic search traffic on your website's conversions and revenue. Track conversion metrics such as leads generated, contact form submissions, e-commerce transactions, and goal completions attributed to organic search traffic. Determine the ROI of your SEO efforts.

8. Monitor User Engagement:

   - Analyze user engagement metrics to assess the quality of organic search traffic. Monitor metrics such as bounce rate, time on page, pages per session, and scroll depth. Identify pages with high engagement and low engagement to optimize content and user experience.

9. Conduct Competitive Analysis:

   - Monitor the SEO performance of your competitors to benchmark your performance and identify areas for improvement. Analyze their keyword rankings, backlink profiles, content strategies, and on-page optimization techniques. Learn from their successes and failures to refine your own SEO strategies.

10. Regularly Review and Adjust Strategies:

   - Regularly review your SEO performance metrics and KPIs to identify trends, patterns, and areas for improvement. Adjust your SEO strategies, tactics, and priorities based on data-driven insights and changes in search engine algorithms or industry trends.

By tracking and analyzing SEO performance using these methods, you can gain valuable insights into the effectiveness of your SEO efforts, make informed decisions about optimization strategies, and ultimately improve your website's visibility, traffic, and conversions from organic search.

Importance of tracking SEO performance metrics to measure success

Tracking SEO performance metrics is crucial for measuring the success of your SEO efforts and achieving your business goals. Here's why it's important:

1. Assess Effectiveness:

Tracking SEO performance metrics allows you to evaluate the effectiveness of your SEO strategies and tactics. By monitoring key metrics such as organic traffic, keyword rankings, and backlink profile, you can determine whether your SEO efforts are generating the desired results.

2. Identify Opportunities:

Analyzing SEO performance metrics helps you identify opportunities for improvement and optimization. By identifying trends, patterns, and areas of underperformance, you can prioritize areas for optimization and focus your efforts on strategies that will yield the greatest impact.

3. Monitor Progress:

Tracking SEO performance metrics allows you to monitor your progress over time. By setting benchmarks and goals for key metrics, you can track your progress towards achieving those goals and make adjustments to your strategies as needed to stay on track.

4. Measure ROI:

SEO is an investment, and tracking performance metrics allows you to measure the return on that investment. By analyzing metrics such as organic traffic, conversion rates, and revenue attributed to organic search, you can determine the ROI of your SEO efforts and justify continued investment in SEO initiatives.

5. Improve Decision Making:

Data-driven decision making is essential for successful SEO. By tracking SEO performance metrics, you can make informed decisions about optimization strategies, content creation, keyword targeting, and resource allocation based on empirical evidence rather than guesswork or intuition.

6. Understand User Behavior:

SEO performance metrics provide insights into user behavior and preferences. By analyzing metrics such as bounce rate, time on page, and pages per session, you can gain a better understanding of how users interact with your website and identify opportunities to improve user experience and engagement.

7. Stay Competitive:

Tracking SEO performance metrics allows you to stay competitive in your industry. By monitoring the SEO performance of your competitors and benchmarking your own performance against theirs, you can identify strengths and weaknesses, learn from their successes and failures, and adapt your strategies accordingly.

8. Adapt to Algorithm Changes:

Search engine algorithms are constantly evolving, and tracking SEO performance metrics allows you to adapt to algorithm changes and updates. By monitoring changes in keyword rankings, organic traffic, and other metrics, you can identify the impact of algorithm updates and adjust your SEO strategies to maintain or improve your search visibility.

In summary, tracking SEO performance metrics is essential for measuring the success of your SEO efforts, identifying opportunities for improvement, monitoring progress towards goals, measuring ROI, making informed decisions, understanding user behavior, staying competitive, and adapting to algorithm changes. By regularly monitoring and analyzing SEO performance metrics, you can optimize your website for search engines, attract more organic traffic, and achieve your business objectives.

Overview of key performance indicators (KPIs) such as website traffic, rankings, and conversions

Key Performance Indicators (KPIs) are measurable metrics that help assess the effectiveness of your SEO efforts and track progress towards your goals.

Here's an overview of key SEO KPIs:

1. Organic Website Traffic

   - **Definition:** The number of visitors who arrive at your website through organic search results on search engines like Google, Bing, or Yahoo.

   - **Importance:** Organic website traffic indicates the visibility and reach of your website in search engine results pages (SERPs). Increasing organic traffic is a primary goal of SEO efforts.

2. Keyword Rankings

   - **Definition:** The positions of your website's pages in search engine results for specific keywords or search queries.

   - **Importance:** Keyword rankings show how well your website is optimized for target keywords and how it performs in search engine rankings. Improving keyword rankings increases visibility and drives organic traffic.

3. Click-Through Rate (CTR)

- **Definition:** The percentage of users who click on your website's link in search engine results out of the total number of users who see the search result (impressions).

- **Importance:** CTR reflects the attractiveness and relevance of your website's titles and meta descriptions in search results. Increasing CTR can lead to higher organic traffic and improved rankings.

4. Bounce Rate

- **Definition:** The percentage of users who leave your website after viewing only one page without interacting further.

- **Importance:** Bounce rate indicates the quality of user experience on your website. A high bounce rate may indicate poor usability, irrelevant content, or slow page load times, which can negatively impact rankings and conversions.

5. Time on Page

- **Definition:** The average amount of time users spend on a specific page of your website.

- **Importance:** Time on page indicates user engagement and interest in your content. Longer time on page suggests that users find your content valuable and engaging, which can positively impact rankings and conversions.

6. Pages per Session

- **Definition:** The average number of pages viewed by users during a single session on your website.

- **Importance:** Pages per session indicate the depth of user engagement and exploration on your website. Increasing pages per session can lead to more opportunities for conversions and higher overall engagement.

7. Conversion Rate

- **Definition:** The percentage of website visitors who complete a desired action, such as making a purchase, filling out a form, or signing up for a newsletter.

- **Importance:** Conversion rate measures the effectiveness of your website in achieving its goals. Improving conversion rate leads to higher ROI and revenue generation from organic traffic.

8. Return on Investment (ROI)

- **Definition:** The ratio of the net profit generated from your SEO efforts to the total cost of those efforts.

- **Importance:** ROI measures the financial impact of your SEO activities. A positive ROI indicates that your SEO efforts are generating value for your business and justifies continued investment in SEO initiatives.

By tracking and analyzing these key performance indicators, you can assess the effectiveness of your SEO efforts, identify areas for improvement, and optimize your website to achieve your business goals.

Tools and techniques for tracking and analyzing SEO performance over time

There are numerous tools and techniques available for tracking and analyzing SEO performance over time. Here are some popular tools and techniques:

1. Google Analytics

   - **Description:** Google Analytics is a powerful web analytics tool that provides insights into website traffic, user behavior, and conversions.

   - **Features:** Track organic traffic, keyword performance, user engagement metrics, conversion rates, and more. Set up custom reports, goals, and segments to analyze SEO performance over time.

   - **Benefits:** Free to use, integrates seamlessly with other Google tools like Google Search Console, provides comprehensive data on website performance.

2. Google Search Console

- **Description:** Google Search Console is a free tool provided by Google that helps monitor and optimize your website's presence in Google search results.

- **Features:** Track keyword rankings, impressions, click-through rates (CTR), and click data. Monitor website errors, indexing status, and mobile usability. Receive alerts for critical issues affecting your website's visibility.

- **Benefits:** Provides valuable insights into how Google perceives your website, identifies opportunities for optimization, and helps diagnose technical issues affecting search performance.

3. SEO Platforms and Software

- **Description:** Various SEO platforms and software offer comprehensive features for tracking and analyzing SEO performance, including keyword rankings, backlink profiles, site audits, and competitor analysis.

- **Examples:** SEMrush, Ahrefs, Moz, SE Ranking, SpyFu, Screaming Frog.

- **Features:** Keyword research, rank tracking, backlink analysis, site audits, competitor analysis, content optimization, and more.

- **Benefits:** Offers advanced features and insights beyond basic analytics tools, facilitates competitive analysis, and streamlines SEO workflow.

4. Rank Tracking Tools

- **Description:** Rank tracking tools allow you to monitor keyword rankings in search engine results pages (SERPs) over time.

- **Examples:** SERPWatcher, AccuRanker, Rank Ranger, Rank Tracker.

- **Features:** Track keyword rankings across multiple search engines and locations. Monitor changes in rankings, identify keyword opportunities, and track competitors' rankings.

- **Benefits:** Provides real-time updates on keyword performance, enables tracking of progress towards SEO goals, and facilitates analysis of ranking trends.

5. Backlink Analysis Tools

- **Description:** Backlink analysis tools help monitor and analyze your website's backlink profile, including the quantity, quality, and diversity of backlinks.

- **Examples:** Ahrefs, Majestic, Moz Link Explorer, SEMrush Backlink Analytics.

- **Features:** Analyze backlink metrics such as domain authority, trust flow, anchor text distribution, and referring domains. Identify new backlink opportunities, monitor competitor backlinks, and disavow harmful links.

- **Benefits:** Provides insights into the authority and credibility of your website, facilitates link building and outreach efforts, and helps protect against negative SEO.

6. Custom Reports and Dashboards

   - **Description:** Create custom reports and dashboards to consolidate and visualize key SEO metrics from multiple sources.

   - **Tools:** Google Data Studio, Microsoft Power BI, Tableau.

   - **Features:** Combine data from Google Analytics, Google Search Console, and other sources. Customize reports with visualizations, charts, and graphs. Schedule automated email reports for stakeholders.

   - **Benefits:** Provides a centralized view of SEO performance metrics, facilitates data-driven decision-making, and enables sharing of insights with team members and clients.

7. Regular Audits and Reviews

   - Conduct regular SEO audits and reviews of your website to identify technical issues, on-page optimization opportunities, and content gaps.

   - Use tools like Screaming Frog, Sitebulb, and DeepCrawl to perform comprehensive site audits and identify areas for improvement.

   - Regularly review performance metrics and KPIs to assess progress towards SEO goals and make data-driven decisions about optimization strategies.

By leveraging these tools and techniques for tracking and analyzing SEO performance over time, you can gain valuable insights into your website's visibility, traffic, and conversions, identify areas for improvement, and optimize your SEO strategies to **achieve your local business success**.

www.ingramcontent.com/pod-product-compliance
Lightning Source LLC
Chambersburg PA
CBHW062226220526
45471CB00009B/3357